# FUTURE TRADING

# THE ULTIMATE DAY AND SWING TRADING STRATEGY FOR ALL TRADERS

Harold Keith

# TABLE OF CONTENT

# INTRODUCTION

Futures are standardized arrangements that address a grasping between two social events, a purchaser and a dealer, to exchange a particular resource at a set cost before a particular end date, called the expiry. Despite what the essential asset's market cost is at the hour of the exchange the expense will stay fixed by the plan. Resources that can be exchanged this way combine bushels of affiliation stocks, items, advance charges, modernized cash, and monetary designs. How much the fundamental not permanently set up in the conceivable outcomes contract. This course is normal for you. Jump into how game plans exchange on a fates trade, the various ways clients utilize these instruments and the advantages that prospects give. Secure a more grounded perception of how fates work and why more market people are remembering subordinates for their exchanging techniques today.Futures Financial exchange: Definition, Model, and How to Exchange, Most essential Day Exchanging Conceivable outcomes Systems Truly Working In 2023,What is a Conceivable outcomes Understanding, Stray bits of Predetermination Exchanging and the sky is the limit starting there.

# CHAPTER ONE

# WHAT IS FUTURES?

Possible results are money related plans in which two social gatherings - one buyer and one dealer - agree to exchange a key market at a respectable cost in the long run not extravagantly far off. Fates give the buyer the obligation to buy the secret market, and the transporter the obligation to sell at or before the strategy's expiry.

With us, you can figure on whether the cost of a fates understanding will rise or fall with CFDs. Since these things are financial partners, you don't have to guess that the responsibility ought to exchange, and won't get a sense of obligation with key asset. Taking into account everything, you will tie down responsiveness to the essential possibilities contract by speculating using CFDs. This concludes that your possible results trades will be used.Impact can work on both your advantages and troubles as they'll be spread out on the full straightforwardness of the trade, in spite of the edge expected to open it. This proposes calamities similarly as advantages could far counterbalance your edge, so reliably ensure you're exchanging inside your means.

**trade with influence**

Potential results contracts are used. That is, they interface with you to get expanded market straightforwardness for a little store - known as edge - and your exchanging provider credits you the rest of the full worth of the exchange.

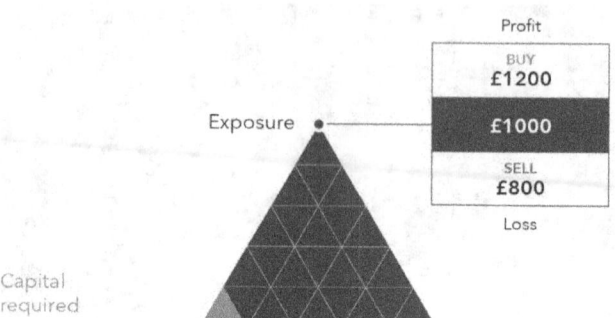

While exchanging with impact, it is significant for review that your advantage or misfortune not completely unfalteringly settled by the full scale size of your circumstance, in spite of the edge used to open it. This assembles there is a trademark bet that you could make an event (or an advantage) that could far balance your mysterious capital cost.

## Access our basic liquidity

How much merchants that we handle constantly - got along with our size, by and large reach and monstrous client base - suggests that our fate markets are particularly liquid. This really suggests that expecting you deal in additional noticeable sizes, you will definitely have your deals filled at your optimal expense.

## Genuinely make an effort not to work with save charges

Transient supporting charges will apply to cash puts that are left open around the completing of a trading day. At any rate, with fates, the current second supporting blame is connected for the spread.This recommends that possibilities trading is loved by individuals who are expecting to take a long situation on a principal market - considering the way that they won't cause different present second supporting charges.

## Go long or short

While exchanging expected results with CFDs, you can go long or short. You'd go long expecting you perceived that the secret market cost will rise, and you'd go short accepting you remembered it will fall.

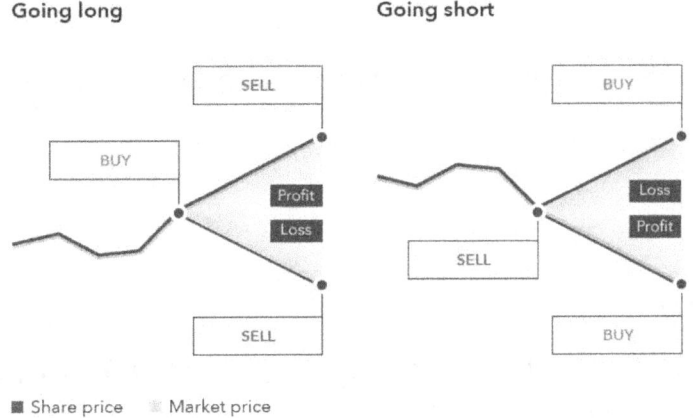

Going long                    Going short

■ Share price    ▪ Market price

With CFDs, your advantage or not really determinedly settled by the precision of your speculation, and the general size of the market improvement.

Support your persistent positions

Supporting with fate engages you to control your responsiveness to bet in a key market. For example, if you own segments in relationship on the FTSE 100 and are stressed over their value dropping, you could short a FTSE 100 record future - the advantages from which would preferably offset a level of your piece position debacles.

Expecting you had current short circumstances clearly, you could go long on a record future in case the market moves, with the likelihood that your long advantages would change your short troubles.

Assemble on incalculable business districts

You can exchange destinies on records, things and bonds with us:

### List futures

Get receptiveness to by and large records including the FTSE 100, Germany 40 and Cash Street.

### Thing possibilities

Keep an eye on both hard and fragile things including gold, silver, wheat, corn and oil.

### Bond prospects

Trade on the value of different bonds rising or falling, including German, UK and US government bonds.

### Fathom how possibilities trading limits

Possible results trading works by using CFDs to figure on the expense of a puzzling destinies market. CFDs can be used to go both long or short, gathering that you can profit from business locales that are moving as well as falling - gave your doubts are correct.

### Pick a possible results market to trade

With various potential results markets to investigate, you should spread out which one is most-fit to your solitary trading style. Two or three records - the Germany 40 for example - experience higher eccentricity than others, and could be more prepared to transient agreeable financial allies.

Different business districts, for instance, gold or silver thing possibilities are oftentimes thoroughly enjoyed by merchants who have lower risk desires and worth business areas with lower eccentricity.

## Make a record and sign in

To start trading destinies with CFDs today, open a record with IG. Our spreads are among the most un-in the business and we have an other destiny offering, which blends the most well known records, things and protections open.

## Pick whether to go long or short

Going long infers that you are speculating on the value of a future extending, and going short suggests that you are assessing on its worth reducing. Expecting you accept that the secret expense of a record, thing or security future will increment contemplating your own head and thought assessment, then, open a long position. Expecting considering everything, your assessment recommends that the key market cost will fall, open a short position.

Place your most crucial trade

## To put your most basic trade,

go to the IG trading stage and select a market. Then, select the 'Possible results' tab on the expense frame, close whether you want to exchange the principal market, and pick your position size.

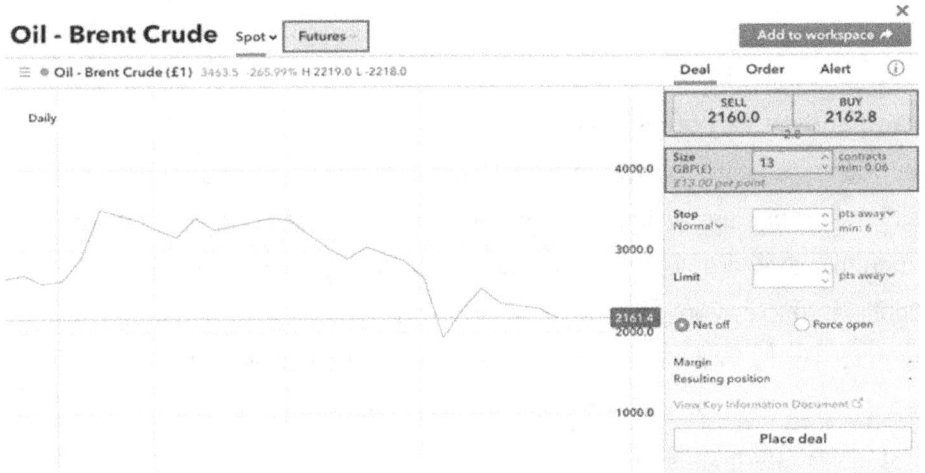

## Put forward your stops and lines

Before you open your situation, you ought to consider adding stops and cutoff points to your exchange. Stops and cutoff points are unequivocally proposed mechanical congregations for dealing with your bet while exchanging potential outcomes.

A stop requesting will close your position in this way if the value moves to a less fair level, while an end sales will close your position ordinarily expecting it moves to a predominant one.

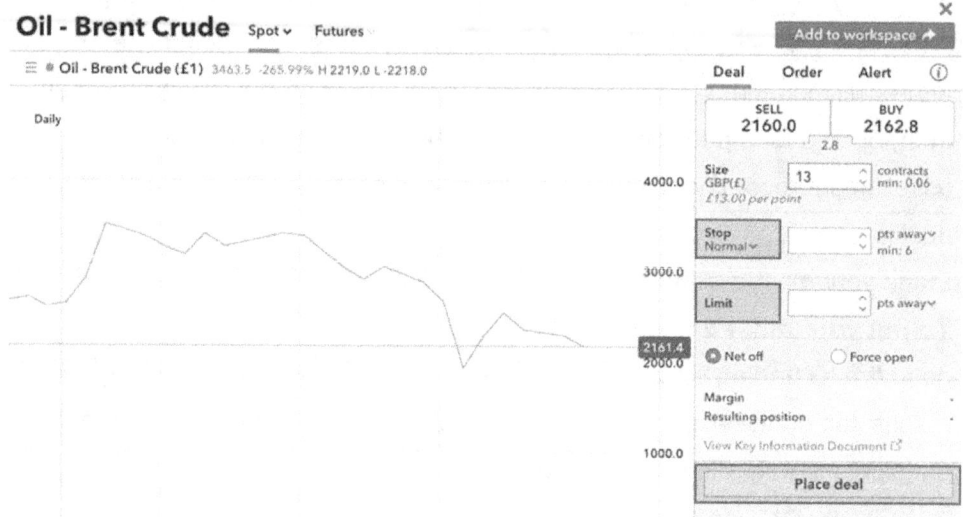

## Screen and close your situation

After you've put your exchange, you'll have to screen it to ensure that the business regions are acting in the manner that you anticipated. On the off chance that they aren't, you should close your exchange to limit your difficulties. In the event that they are, you should close your exchange straightforwardly following enjoying accomplished a fair benefit.

Keep in mind, you can close a fates contract exchange before the expiry date of the comprehension shows up.

## Potential outcomes contract exchanging model

With cash related subordinates, for example, CFDs, you'll guess on the worth upgrades of a predetermination contract rather than trading the certified comprehension.

Could we acknowledge it's April and you figure the cost of oil will ascend from here on

out - you could open a long CFD on a June oil future. Your not totally forever settled by how much the cost of oil has move by the future's expiry, and the size of your situation - less any charges. These will incorporate your spread and at least a couple expenses or charges.

Of course, expecting you acknowledge that the cost of oil will fall, you could go short with a CFD on the oil future. In this model, you'd help thinking about how much the oil cost fell and the size of your situation (less the spread total) and any expenses caused.

In the two conditions, your position would be shut ordinarily in June - yet you could close it as of now on the off chance that you truly cared about. Under, you'll see a sensible of the potential outcomes tab in IG's exchanging stage. Expecting you felt that the crucial market cost planned to rise, you'd purchase the market on your CFD exchanging account. Expecting you felt that urgent market cost planned to fall, you'd sell.

The months for a fates understanding will move, and the model given here which utilizes June is for edifying inspirations. You ought to check the expiry of a predetermination contract before you open a position

# CHAPTER TWO

# HOW DOES FUTURES TRADING WORKS

Possibilities work by getting in the continuous business area cost and setting it as the respectable expense at which a secret asset will be exchanged later on. At some point not excessively far off - at the extremely most recent expiry of the arrangement - the market cost, likely, will be one of a kind. The settled upon cost would then be either higher or lower than the new market cost.

If the new market cost is higher than the possibilities contract esteem, the buyer benefits as they'll get a good deal on the secret asset. While, expecting the new market cost is lower than in the game plan, the seller benefits since they'll be finished more than the continuous expense per measure of the asset. Clearly, where the one party benefits, different passes up a major opportunity.

There are three head sorts of future dealers:
- ☐**Inspectors** take what is happening on the direction of an asset's expense improvement - most retail sellers fall under this future representative sort
- ☐Creators (hedgers) plan to limit their bet by getting in expenses of expected creation (stock they creation like oil, gold and wheat)
- ☐Position holders keep their trades open for a broad stretch of time (could be anything among weeks and years)

The definition and elements of destinies go against a well known assumption that everything spins around predicting what's to come on the money related business areas. As wonderful as that would be, you're really estimating on looming esteem improvements and there's actual limit with respect to help expecting all works out positively.

**Buying instead of SELLING Possibilities**

The principal thought of buying and a short time later selling is a normally known thought in the domain of trading. On the back of this, you can buy destinies contracts (or go long on them) with believes that the essential asset it covers appreciates, so you can offer it at a more noteworthy expense to make an increase. In any case, you can similarly auction possibilities contracts on the opportunity that you figure the fundamental asset will disintegrate - generally called going short. You'd then repurchase it (or cover it) at a lower cost to obtain an advantage.

A commonplace request among those new to shorting is, 'the way could you sell something you don't guarantee?' When you are the vendor of a destinies contract, you agree to sell the principal asset soon, at the possibilities contract cost.

In outline, while going long, you want to benefit by selling the asset at a more excessive expense. You'd close a long circumstance to sell it. Then again, you want to benefit by closing your short circumstance at a lower cost while going short. To close a short position, you ought to buy (or cover) it.

**Possibilities Arrangements Standardization**

Liquidity is ensured in possibilities contracts through standardization - setting a definite benchmark on different factors considering the principal asset. This is done by outlining subtleties, for instance,

The essential asset: the particular asset, for instance box of stocks, items

- ☐Reimbursement type: cash reimbursement or genuine transport
- ☐Contract unit: how much the fundamental asset peddled in one arrangement, for instance 1,000 barrels of crude oil
- ☐Cash: the money of the destinies understanding's expense reference

- Quality: the grade of the basic resource
- Date of conveyance: when the last money repayment, or the conveyance, will be made
- Last exchanging date: the day preceding the expiry date of the agreement
- Tick size and worth: the additions by which costs can change and its worth, for example the tick size for unrefined petroleum is 0.01 and the tick esteem is $10
- Greatest cost vacillation allowed: cost limit that is permitted inside an exchanging meeting

## Fates Agreement Model

A fates contract incorporates some vital data as illustrated in the underneath model. This incorporates:

- Item: the sort of basic resource, for example unrefined petroleum is a ware
- Termination: the day on which the agreement closes
- Amount: contract unit, for example 1,000
- Value: the settled upon cost of the prospects contract

# Marking to Market

**Two Parties**

 **Enters a Futures contract of cotton at $150**

**Party A**          **Next day as price increased**          **Party B**
(Trader in short position will collect from long position.)

**If the mark to market price falls**

**MARK-TO-MARKET IN Fates**

Prospects and choices on fates are set apart to-showcase consistently as indicated by the exchanging day's settlement cost. Hence, the IRS alludes to these as a Part 1256 items.

Mark-to-showcase is a money term - thus, it isn't restrictive to exchanging. With respect to prospects contracts, stamping to-showcase is a method of esteeming resources toward the finish of each exchanging day, when benefits and misfortunes are settled among long and short positions.

This approach to estimating fair worth as per market cost truly intends that, with the adjustment of worth of the agreement every day, a settlement will be made to mirror this.

We should place this into setting...

**MARK-TO-MARKET IN Fates Exchanging Model**

Since a purchaser is basically bullish and a merchant is negative, a lower cost by the day's end would mean a misfortune for the long position and an increase for the short position. The purchaser and dealer's records are refreshed day to day (aggregate addition or misfortune) in light of this until the lapse, or when the position is shut.

The adjustment of significant worth from the prospects cost, as well as the heading, decides gains and misfortunes. The party with the place that matches bearing of the adjustment of significant worth will gather the distinction in esteem (from the prospects cost) toward the finish of every day, while different makes a misfortune identical to the adjustment of significant worth. Nonetheless, hidden misfortunes might be considered in once the position has been shut.

# WHY TRADE FUTURES

## TRANSPARENT PRICING & FEES

## CAPITAL EFFICIENCY

Spending plan for your positions precisely early and open a situation from as low as $0.25 commission

## NEAR ROUND-THE-CLOCK MONITORING

Take your capital further, with higher potential returns, using leverage; including increased accessibility with <u>the smalls</u>

Experience adaptability - 23 hours accessibility every day implies you can design prospects exchanging around your life

## BROAD RANGE OF MARKETS

Investigate our fates item reach and take a pick - you can get to the perfect times for you

## GO LONG OR SHORT

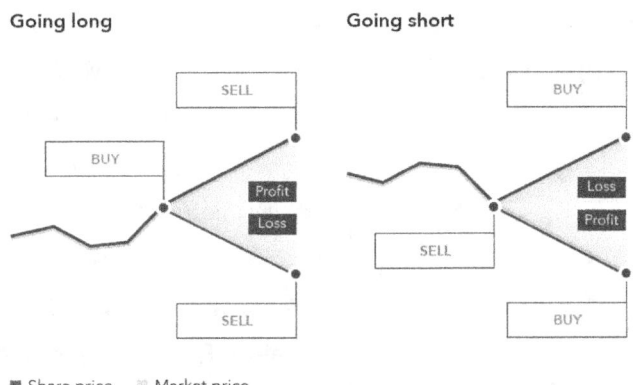

Estimate on both rising and falling costs - in light of the fact that occasionally 'the best way to go is up' is only a choice

## HIGH LIQUIDITY

Appreciate more noteworthy productivity with tight spreads and many agreements on the two sides of the market

**TYPES OF FUTURES**

| TYPES | Futures products you can trade with tasty works |
|---|---|
| **Value Record Prospects** Assortments of stocks in a value record offer a sign of how an area, trade or an economy is performing. Accordingly, value record prospects can give you wide openness. | <ul><li>E-small S&P 500 (/ES)</li><li>Miniature E-small S&P 500 (/MES)</li><li>E-small Nasdaq 100 (/NQ)</li><li>Miniature E-small NASDAQ 100 (/MNQ)</li><li>E-smaller than usual Dow 30 (/YM)</li><li>Miniature E-smaller than usual DOW (/MYM)</li><li>E-small Russell 2000 (/RTY)</li></ul>Miniature E-small Russell 2000 (/M2K) |
| **Loan cost Fates** Changes in loan fee, the expense for getting, can be brought about by different variables. You can estimate on these developments on | <ul><li>Long term T-Note (/ZT)</li><li>Long term T-Note (/ZF)</li><li>Long term T-Note (/ZN)</li><li>Long term T-Bond (/ZB)</li><li>multi Day Eurodollar (/GE)</li><li>Miniature 2-Year Yield (/2YY)</li></ul> |

| | |
|---|---|
| unambiguous obligation instruments. | <ul><li>Miniature 5-Year Yield (/5YY)</li><li>Miniature 10-Year Yield (/10Y)</li><li>Miniature 30-Year Yield (/30Y)</li></ul>Ultra U.S. Depository Bonds (/UB) |
| **Unfamiliar Money Fates**<br><br>The worth of one money against another is consistently evolving. With<br><br>solid impacts that become an integral factor, for example twofold occasions, international relations, and global relations, you can uphold your theory with some genuine activity and verifiable information | <ul><li>Euro FX (/6E)</li><li>Miniature Euro (/M6E)</li><li>Japanese Yen (/6J)</li><li></li><li>Miniature Japanese Yen (/MJY)</li><li>English Pound (/6B)</li><li>Miniature English Pound (/M6B)</li><li>Canadian Dollar (/6C)</li><li>Miniature Canadian Dollar (/MCD)</li><li>Australian Dollar (/6A)</li></ul>Miniature Australian Dollar (/M6A) |
| **Instability Fates**<br>Expanded relative development of market costs accompanies more open doors for progress. Unpredictability fates empower you to take positions in view of a bin of stocks' normal hazardousness in cost. | <ul><li>CBOE Instability Record (VIX) Fates (/VX)</li></ul>CBOE Scaled down Instability List (VIX) Fates (/VX |
| <ul><li>CBOE Instability Record (VIX) Fates (/VX)</li></ul>CBOE Scaled down Instability List (VIX) Fates (/VX | Bitcoin (/BTC)<br>Miniature Bitcoin (/MBT) |
| **Item Prospects**<br>Hard and delicate items have been a bedrock of approaches to living across hundreds of years all through the world. You can take a situation on these normal assets that have seen days of yore travel every which way. | |

**Energy**

- Raw petroleum (/CL)
- Miniature Raw petroleum (/MCL)
- E-small scale Unrefined petroleum (/QM)
- Henry Center Petroleum gas (/NG)
- E-small scale Petroleum gas (/QG)

**Metals**

Gold (/GC)
- Miniature Gold (/MGC)

Copper (/HG)
- Silver (/SI)
- Miniature Silver (/SIL)

**Farming**

- Corn Fates (/ZC)
- Little Corn (/XC)
- Soybean (/ZS)
- Little Soybean (/XK)
- Chicago SRW Wheat (/ZW)

Little Chicago SRW Wheat (/XW)

## WHAT IS Fates Exchanging AND HOW Can IT Function?

Fates exchanging is sincerely promising to take a situation by a future date, either trading a particular basic resource, at a foreordained, fixed cost. It works by having a prospects contract set up that is placed into by a purchaser and a vender, who both have a commitment to keep their word.

Dive more deeply into fates exchanging

While a fates agreement can shield you from negative cost transforms, you likewise risk passing up a superior cost. It's not precisely go big or go home, or a mutually beneficial arrangement - however some in the middle between.

We should have a more critical gander at this when placed into setting.

## NOTIONAL Worth AND Influence IN Fates Exchanging

Notional worth is the all out worth of the fundamental resource that is controlled in a subsidiaries exchange, for example the sum you stand to lose. It does exclude extra expenses like commission and edge alleviation. Purchasing power can change in light of the position and market unpredictability. That is the reason you don't just need your underlying edge sum, which is utilized to open your prospects position, yet you additionally need support edge. This is the base sum required in your record at some random time. An edge call happens on the off chance that the sum in your record is not exactly the support edge.

Notional worth is determined by increasing the spot cost with the fates contract size, or number of units of the basic resource. We should go on with our illustration of a 1,000 raw petroleum barrels fates contract at a cost of $75.72 per barrel ($75.72 x 1,000). The notional worth in danger for this situation is $75,720.00.

Market esteem contrasts from the notional worth - it's the spot cost of the hidden resource per unit, or the fates contract cost. According to the model, the market worth of unrefined petroleum is $75.72.

Further, influence immensely affects your exchanging. It implies that you just need to commit a specific level of the full worth of the exchange forthright. Regardless of advancing less at first, your gamble continues as before for long positions - the notional worth. On the off chance that you went short on a prospects contract, notwithstanding, your gamble isn't covered.

## Fates Agreement TICK SIZE

In subordinates exchanging, an agreement's tick size is the littlest addition by which costs of the fundamental resource can vary. A trade sets the tick size for an instrument. On the Chicago Commercial Trade (CME), the tick size for unrefined petroleum is 0.01 and each point is valued at $1,000. Duplicating these two qualities gives you the tick esteem - which, for this situation is $10 (ticks to a point).

Focuses are on the left half of the decimal mark of a cost and ticks are on the right.

Assuming the cost of raw petroleum climbs 25 ticks (0.01 x 25) from the spot cost in the model ($75.72), it would then become $75.97. That could appear to be unimportant - however duplicated by the tick size ($10), it represents a $250 change in your benefit or misfortune.

This implies you stand to acquire $250 on the off chance that you went long, or lose $250 assuming you took a short position. On the off chance that you took a situation on numerous fates contracts, you'd increase this worth by the quantity of agreements.

## Fates Exchanging Model

Fates exchanging ranges from the time the agreement is placed (otherwise called 'opened') to the time the position is left (otherwise called 'shut'), or when this occurs as a matter of course at lapse. In the event that the market cost is higher when the trade is made, you'd benefit on the off chance that you took a long position (purchasing), and the merchant would miss out.

Then again, when the market cost is lower than the prospects contract foreordained set cost would help the dealer and the purchaser would miss out.

Assume you purchase a raw petroleum fates agreement and you've consented to buying 1,000 barrels of it at a cost of $75.72 by September 22nd. In the event that the cost of unrefined petroleum drops and stays low after you enter the understanding, you'll cause a misfortune on the off chance that this is as yet the situation at termination. Yet, on the off chance that it transcends the prospects cost, you'd create a gain.

One way or the other, you actually get an opportunity to attempt to secure in benefits or breaking point misfortunes before the expiry date. In the event that the market moves against your situation, you can open and close it whenever - there are no example day exchanging (PDT) rules for fates, as they aren't protections. This is valuable when you need to change your directional suspicion in a specific fates item.

**Prospects Versus Choices: WHAT ARE THE Distinctions?**

Prospects and choices vary in more than one way. You could ask yourself which is better among prospects and choices. These include:

| FUTURES | OPTIONS |
|---|---|
| Commitment to trade | Right while purchasing, commitment while selling |
| No premium and likelihood of benefit is fifty (straight result) - relies upon course as it were | An exceptional applies (purchasers pay and merchants gather) and openness is non-direct |

Choices and prospects may be apples and oranges, yet they are additionally comparative here and there, for example both are monetary subsidiaries that can utilized for support. Both likewise empower an exchange to be made at a future cost and by a specific date.

## Choices ON Prospects: WHAT ARE THEY AND HOW Would THEY Function?

Dissimilar to their value choice partner, which is attached to 100 portions of stock, choices on prospects are choices that are attached to a solitary fates contract. It's a subsidiary of a subordinate. Essentially, the worth of the choice sticks to every prospects contract tick esteem.

Like their value choice partner, purchasers of choices on prospects give the option to trade the hidden fates contract at the strike; and merchants of choices on fates have the commitment to trade the fundamental future at the strike cost.

Subtleties that are regularly remembered for a choice on prospects contract are the item, the future's agreement month, and the set cost to trade the fates contract.

**Instructions to Begin Exchanging Fates**

- Investigate as needs be to get a comprehension of how fates exchanging functions
- Make a record or sign in
- Pick your favored market and resource
- Make an exchanging plan and deal with your gamble
- Open your fates position and screen it
- Close your situation if you have any desire to do as such before the agreement expires1

# CHAPTER THREE

# FUTURES IN STOCK MARKET DEFINITION; EXAMPLE AND HOW TO TRADE

## What Are futures?

Futures are subsidiary monetary agreements that commit gatherings to trade a resource at a foreordained future date and cost. The purchaser should buy or the dealer should sell the hidden resource at the set value, no matter what the ongoing business sector cost at the termination date.

Hidden resources incorporate actual wares and monetary instruments. Prospects contracts detail the amount of the hidden resource and are normalized to work with exchanging on a fates trade. Prospects can be utilized for supporting or exchange hypothesis.

## KEY Action items

- Fates are subsidiary monetary agreements committing the purchaser to buy a resource or the merchant to sell a resource at a foreordained future date and set cost.
- A fates contract permits a financial backer to estimate on the cost of a monetary instrument or ware.
- Fates are utilized to fence the value development of a basic resource for assist with keeping misfortunes from troublesome cost changes.
- At the point when you participate in supporting, you take a situation inverse to the one you hold with the fundamental resource; on the off chance that you lose cash on the basic resource, the cash you make on the fates agreement can moderate that misfortune.
- Prospects contracts exchange on a fates trade and an agreement's cost settles after the finish of each and every exchanging meeting.

## Grasping Prospects

Prospects — likewise called fates contracts — permit merchants to secure in the cost of the hidden resource or product. These agreements have lapse dates and set costs that are known forthright. Prospects are recognized by their termination month. For instance, a December gold prospects contract terminates in December.

Brokers and financial backers utilize the term fates concerning the general resource class. Notwithstanding, there are many sorts of fates contracts accessible for exchanging including:

- Product fates with basic wares like raw petroleum, flammable gas, corn, and wheat
- Stock list fates with basic resources like the S&P 500 Record
- Money fates including those for the euro and the English pound
- Valuable metal prospects for gold and silver

- U.S. Depository prospects for bonds and other monetary protections

Taking note of the qualification among choices and futures is significant. American-style choices contracts give the holder the right (however not the commitment) to trade the hidden resource any time before the lapse date of the agreement. With European choices, you can practice at lapse however don't need to practice that right.

The purchaser of a fates contract, then again, is committed to claim the hidden item (or the monetary same) at the hour of termination and no time previously. The purchaser of a prospects agreement can sell their situation whenever before lapse and be liberated from their commitment. Along these lines, purchasers of the two choices and prospects contracts benefit from an influence holder's position shutting before the lapse date.

**Experts**

- Financial backers can utilize fates agreements to hypothesize on the heading of the cost of a fundamental resource.
- Organizations can support the cost of their unrefined components or items they offer to safeguard against unfavorable cost developments.
- Fates agreements may just require a store of a small part of the agreement sum with an intermediary.

**Cons**

- Financial backers risk losing more than the underlying edge sum since fates use influence.
- Putting resources into a fates agreement could cause an organization that supported to pass up positive cost developments.
- Edge can be a two sided deal, importance gains are intensified however so too are misfortunes.

**Utilizing Fates**

The fates showcases regularly utilize high influence. Influence implies that the broker doesn't have to set up 100 percent of the agreement's worth sum while going into an exchange. All things being equal, the intermediary would require an underlying edge sum, which comprises of a small part of the complete agreement esteem

**NOTE;** The sum expected by the merchant for an edge record can shift contingent upon the size of the fates contract, the financial soundness of the financial backer, and the specialist's agreements

The trade where the prospects contract exchanges will decide whether the agreement is for actual conveyance or on the other hand on the off chance that it very well may be cash-settled. A company might go into an actual conveyance agreement to secure in the cost of a ware it needs for creation. In any case, numerous fates contracts include merchants who conjecture on the exchange. These agreements are finished off or gotten — the distinction in the first exchange and shutting exchange cost — and have a money repayment.

**Prospects for Hypothesis**

A prospects contract permits a dealer to guess on the heading of an item's cost. On the off chance that a dealer purchased a prospects contract and the cost of the product transcended the first agreement cost at lapse, then they would have a benefit. Before lapse, the prospects contract — the long position — would be sold at the ongoing cost, shutting the long position.

The contrast between the costs would be cash-gotten comfortable the financial backer's money market fund, and no actual item would change hands. Notwithstanding, the merchant could likewise lose assuming the item's cost was lower than the price tag determined in the fates contract. Examiners can likewise take a short speculative position on the off chance that they foresee the cost of the fundamental resource will fall. Assuming that the cost declines, the merchant will take a counterbalancing position to close the agreement. Once more, the net contrast would be settled at the termination of the agreement. A financial backer would understand an increase on the off chance that the hidden resource's cost was beneath the agreement cost and a misfortune assuming that the ongoing cost was over the agreement cost. It's critical to take note of that exchanging on edge considers a lot bigger situation than the sum held by the money market fund. Subsequently, edge financial planning can enhance gains, however it can likewise amplify misfortunes.

Envision a dealer who has a $5,000 money market fund total and has a $50,000 position in raw petroleum. Assuming the cost of oil moves against the exchange, it can mean misfortunes that far surpass the record's $5,000 beginning edge sum. For this situation, the specialist would settle on an edge decision expecting that extra assets be stored to cover the market misfortunes.

## Prospects for Supporting

Prospects can be utilized to support the value development of the hidden resource. Here, the objective is to keep misfortunes from possibly ominous cost changes instead of to estimate. Many organizations that enter supports are utilizing — or generally speaking creating — the fundamental resource.

For instance, corn ranchers can utilize fates to secure in a particular cost for selling their corn crop. Thusly, they diminish their gamble and assurance they will get the decent cost. In the event that the cost of corn diminished, the rancher would have an increase on the support to balance misfortunes from selling the corn at the market. With such an increase and misfortune balancing one another, the supporting really secures in a satisfactory market cost.

## Illustration of Fates

Suppose a dealer needs to estimate on the cost of raw petroleum by going into a fates contract in May with the assumption that the cost will be higher by year-end. The December unrefined petroleum prospects contract is exchanging at $50 and the merchant purchases the agreement.

Since oil is exchanged additions of 1,000 barrels, the financial backer presently has a position worth $50,000 of raw petroleum (1,000 x $50 = $50,000).

In any case, the merchant will just have to pay a small part of that sum front and center — the underlying edge that they store with the dealer.

From May to December, the cost of oil changes as does the worth of the prospects contract. Assuming oil's cost gets too unpredictable, the dealer might have to request that that extra assets be kept into the edge account. This is called upkeep edge.

In December, the end date of the agreement is drawing nearer (the third Friday of the month). The cost of unrefined petroleum has ascended to $65. The merchant offers the first agreement to leave the position. The net distinction is cash-settled. They procure $15,000, less any expenses and commissions owed the agent ($65 - $50 = $15 x 1000 = $15,000).

Be that as it may, on the off chance that the cost oil had tumbled to $40 all things considered, the financial backer would have lost $10,000 ($50 - $40 = a deficiency of $10 x 1000 = a deficiency of $10,000).

## What Are Fates Agreements?

Fates contracts are a speculation vehicle that permits the purchaser to wager on the future cost of a product or other security. There are many kinds of prospects contracts accessible. These may have fundamental resources like oil, securities exchange files, monetary standards, and farming items.

Not at all like forward agreements, which are redone between the gatherings in question, prospects contracts exchange on coordinated trades, for example, those worked by the CME Gathering Inc. (CME). Prospects contracts are famous among dealers, who plan to benefit on cost swings, as well as business clients who wish to support their dangers.

## Are Fates a Kind of Subordinate?

Indeed, fates contracts are a kind of subsidiary item. They are subordinates on the grounds that their worth depends on the worth of a hidden resource, like oil on account of raw petroleum fates. In the same way as other subsidiaries, fates are a utilized monetary instrument, offering the potential for outsized additions or misfortunes. Thusly, they are by and large viewed as a high level exchanging instrument and are generally exchanged simply by experienced financial backers and foundations.

What Occurs on the off chance that You Hold a Prospects Agreement Until Termination?
Regularly, brokers who hold prospects contracts until termination will settle their situation in real money. As such, the broker will just compensation or get a money repayment relying upon whether the fundamental resource expanded or diminished during the speculation holding period.

At times, nonetheless, prospects agreements will require actual conveyance. In this situation, the financial backer holding the agreement upon lapse would take conveyance of the fundamental resource. They'd be liable for the merchandise and taking care of expenses for material dealing with, actual capacity, and protection.

# CHAPTER FOUR

# BEST DAY TRADING FUTURES STRATEGIES STILL WORKING IN 2023

Destinies are popular assets among casual financial backers and colossal institutional monetary patrons. A destinies contract insinuates a grasping between two people. In this getting it, the buyer will commitment to buy an asset soon and at a particular expense. Also, the vendor will be supposed to give the asset at the agreed expense.

This is adequate to fathom the colossal qualification between this asset and common stocks, which are influenced dynamically by news and other various things. This qualification is similarly seen in the strategies to be taken on, since they are plainly altered another way.

In this article, we will look at a piece of the top strategies to trade possibilities. Anyway a couple of central considerations that it, in particular, is perfect to have clear at the highest point of the need list.

**Prospects MARKET DEFINITION**

The destinies market is a reasonably standard market that began in the cultivating region. The idea is direct. In case you are a corn farmer, you can go into a simultaneous with a buyer.

The buyer can promise to buy your corn at $1,000 when you gather it. This trade will give you genuine tranquility since you will have a trustworthy buyer for your produce. Regardless, while the buyer has a choice to buy, they don't have a guarantee to buy the corn.

Today, the destinies market runs the universe of items. By and large, representatives make deals using the possibilities market. A piece of various kinds of possibilities market are in:

- ☐Stocks
- ☐Records
- ☐Advance expenses
- ☐Metals
- ☐Woods

☐Tamed creatures

additionally, some more.

Beforehand, possibilities contracts were filled in the real market. This has changed lately and the connection is significantly robotized.

A certified outline of a possibilities market is in records. If you are a sharp crowd of financial media, you have likely heard the eyewitnesses imply record possibilities before the standard gathering. This happens since the possibilities market is ordinarily open for longer hours than the standard gathering.

Another veritable outline of a destinies contract is the one introduced by the CME Social event. This is comparative destinies contract that is trailed by the BITO ETF.

Irrefutably the best possibilities exchanges the US are the Chicago Driving gathering of Trade and CME.

**Destinies Trading Frameworks**

There are various destinies trading frameworks that you can use the market. A piece of these frameworks are:

- ☐Design following
- ☐Reversals
- ☐

- Scalping
- ☐Trade

☐Channel trading strategy

Permit us to immediately look at all of these procedures.

**Design Following**

In design following, you revolve around exchanging assets that have recently settled a model. For this present circumstance, in case a stock destinies is rising, you get it and benefit as the expense rises.

Likewise, if the expense is falling, you short it and benefit as it declines. You can use an example pointer like moving ordinary to recognize where the example will end.

For example, the diagram under shows Dow Jones destinies with a 25-day moving ordinary. For this present circumstance, the bullish example will continue however lengthy it is over this Mom.

**Reversals**

Second, you can use the reversals methodology. This is where the asset is moving in a bullish or negative example and a while later you enter a trade believing that it will switch. There are a couple of ways of managing this. You can use markers, candle plans like Doji and overpowering, and diagram plans like wedges and head and shoulders.

**Channels**

Third, you can trade destinies using the channel framework. This is where you separate a level or inclining channel and keep it together for a breakout.

One of the most astounding ways of managing this is to use approaching requests. This is where you place a blend of an exchange stop and subsequently shield them using a stop incident and a take-benefit.

**Tip: Standing firm on Tractions Until the Next Day is Dangerous**

Furthermore called going long on destinies, standing firm on footings present moment could possibly cause you to lose cash. The possibilities could close toward the day's end at one expense and open the next day at an altogether unique expense.

Casual financial backers who close out their positions reliably don't have to worry about losing cash when the market opens in the initial segment of the day. this strategy is an indispensable trading methodology.

**Advantages and disadvantages**

As made sense of, in destinies trading frameworks the advantages are high upon right gauge. Another benefit of this trade is related with the liquidity of the business areas.

Orders in these procedures can be put quickly, making the cultivated monetary supporters get their money fast. At last, commissions in the trade are less when stood out from various kinds of hypothesis.

**Learning Day Trading Takes Longer-Assumption to learn and adjust**

It expects venture to learn about future trading approaches day trading.

Position shippers could make simply a solitary trade reliably, yet casual financial backers habitually make many trades reliably.

The times you go into trades consistently makes it harder to acknowledge what you need to acknowledge about day trading.**Pick a Liquid Market in Which to Trade**

Various casual financial backers like to include the E-downsized S&P 500 market for trading possibilities. Since the trading that market is electronic, the E-little S&P partakes in the advantage of offering trades that are very speedy and liquid.

E-limited scope Nasdaq possibilities, E-little Russell destinies and Dow destinies are a part of various business areas, and each market has different features.

# CHAPTER FIVE

# WHAT IS A FUTURES CONTRACT

A conceivable outcomes contract is a lawful understanding through an arranged trade to trade a specific resource or thing at a predetermined cost at this point conveyed and paid for on a future date

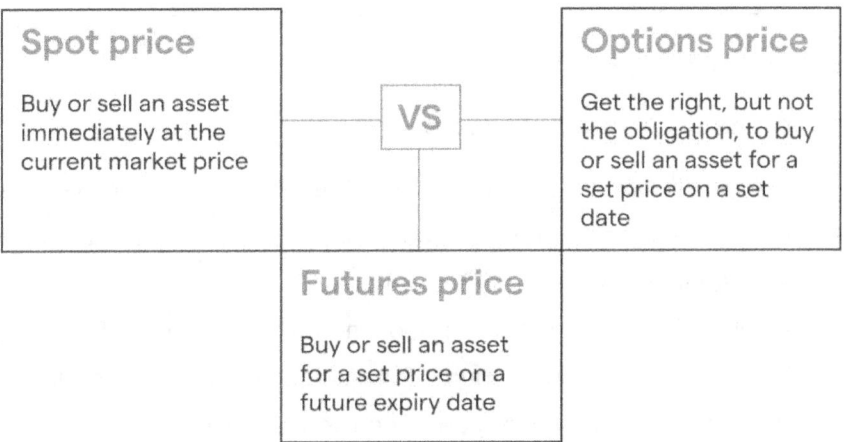

Conceivable outcomes exchanging is just the trade among purchasers and broker of these courses of action.

New merchants hear this definition and get terrified/confused about "paid for on a future date". I guarantee that there's little separation between day exchanging a conceivable outcomes contract versus stocks.

**History of Conceivable outcomes Game plans**

Future plans have been around for quite a while. They can be followed very far back to 1750 BCE in Mesopotamia, organized in present-day Iraq!

# History of Futures

- ☆ **Japan**
    - ☆ Started in Japan in early 1700s with Rice Futures
- ☆ **Chicago**
    - ☆ But it wasn't until the mid-19th century that the true birth of the modern futures markets and futures contracts began
    - ☆ Chicago Board of Trade (CBOT) was established in 1848
- ☆ **Financial Futures**
    - ☆ Financial Futures started in 70s.

Comparable courses of action can be viewed as alluded to in the Hammurabi Code (over), perhaps of the most settled translated sythesis on earth found in Babylonian authentic text made 1755-1750 BC.

The essential for fates contracts emerged whenever two social affairs expected to trade a decent or resource for a settled upon cost sooner or later not unnecessarily distant. To safeguard the two players in the exchange there should have been a made comprehension. Thusly, future plans were envisioned.

The fundamental power fates trade the Bound together State was the Chicago Driving social affair of Exchange (CBOT) which opened in 1848. The head potential outcomes contracts exchanged were corn, wheat, and soybeans.

**Who Exchanges Prospects**

Future traders can be portrayed into two parties, hedgers and experts

Hedgers use the potential results market to supervise respect chance of something given.

In our model from earlier, both the plane connection and the oil producer were supporting against any goliath pushes ahead with the expense of oil, hence both would be seen as hedgers.

Inspectors are delegates who see the expense risk attempting to profit from remarkable expense improvement. Specialists give by a long shot a large portion of liquidity in the possible results markets. Thusly this licenses hedgers to enter and leave the business locales in a more capable manner. Administrators are involved full time talented vendors, inconsequential individual merchants trading their own resources (like yourself), portfolio pioneers, and hypothetical corporate offers.

**Utilizing Conceivable outcomes to Fence Chance**

To show the real diversion for the potential results market, consider the plane business and the cost of stream fuel.

Southwest Planes needs to get in fly fuel expenses to avoid an unanticipated progression in oil costs (Hedger). Likely arrangements give Southwest the ability to get in fuel costs for improvement at a future picked date.

Particularly like Southwest, a fuel producer could find it obliging to help against the decline in the expense of oil allowing them to ensure they can remain significant if oil costs were to drop.

The producer offers a destinies consent to ensure security from an astonishing decreasing in costs.

The different sides pick unambiguous terms: To exchange 10 million gallons of fuel, conveying it in 90 days, at an expense of $40 per gallon.

Southwest Transporters did this during the 2000's, making them one of few **planes to remain strong as oil costs took off.**

Stray bits of Conceivable outcomes Exchanging

Trading potential results isn't exceptionally not precisely comparable to another security, you generally need to sort out a couple of the vagabond pieces. We ought to start by looking at the fundamentals of a destinies contract.

**Contract Size** - Every future understanding has an ordained size that doesn't change. For example, the E-more genuine than ordinary S&P 500 destinies contract size is all over $50 times the expense of the outline. Choices for all possibilities contracts traded at the Chicago Business Exchange (CME)

**Contract Worth** - The perception worth of a possible results plan not absolutely decidedly settled by copying the arrangement size by the perpetual expense of the subordinate. For example, the E-little S&P 500 has an arrangement size of $50. If the perpetual expense of the ES (E-limited scope S&P 500) is $2,905.00 then the arrangement regard is $50 times $2,905.00 which approaches $145,250.

**Tick Size** - The base worth improvement of a possible results contract is assessed in ticks. For you Forex shippers a tick seems to be a pip. Tick size will change starting with one seeing then onto the accompanying.
A tick on the ES (E-little S&P 500) is commensurate to one-fourth of a record point. Since a record point is respected at $50 on the ES, one tick is obscure from $12.50.

**Kinds of Future Strategies**

The destinies market has expanded shockingly since the typical creating things began trading on the floor. At last dealers approach different business areas including:

- □□□Plant Fates: at first began at the Chicago Business Exchange (CME). Joins grain, fibers, screw up, milk, coffee, sugar and even creatures
- □□□Energy Possibilities: Consolidations standard vivifies like bothersome and ignitable gas.
- □□□Metal Possibilities: Present day metals, similar to gold, steel, and copper.
- □□□Cash Destinies: Give receptiveness to changes in the exchange rates

additionally, supporting expenses of public money related norms

☐☐Cash related Possible results: Vix Destinies, Record Possibilities, and Fortune Possibilities

☐With a conclusive objective of this accomplice, we will focus in on Synopsis Possibilities, as it's where I remember anyone new to trading destinies should begin.

## Stock Once-over Possibilities

| weekday starting Monday 1 | 1 | 2 | 3 | 4 | 5 | 6 | 7 | 8 | 9 | 10 | 11 | 12 |
|---|---|---|---|---|---|---|---|---|---|---|---|---|
| 2 | 357.41 | 401.67 | 341.78 | 333.19 | 347.43 | 296.00 | 483.36 | 513.72 | 469.01 | 438.53 | 426.32 | 388.74 |
| 3 | 338.42 | 414.38 | 376.65 | 357.68 | 360.85 | 372.98 | 492.66 | 437.43 | 415.79 | 393.88 | 378.70 | 419.99 |
| 4 | 381.84 | 409.10 | 365.54 | 333.85 | 361.77 | 360.78 | 478.57 | 460.72 | 453.95 | 400.95 | 449.09 | 410.78 |
| 5 | 332.48 | 393.80 | 373.26 | 394.30 | 346.65 | 359.13 | 499.62 | 428.02 | 386.84 | 347.67 | 453.29 | 374.28 |
| 6 | 312.84 | 437.67 | 359.86 | 314.22 | 313.85 | 361.36 | 549.20 | 517.04 | 355.85 | 441.94 | 458.01 | 330.00 |

| Day of Week Name | April | August | December | February | January | July | June | March | May | November | October | September |
|---|---|---|---|---|---|---|---|---|---|---|---|---|
| Friday | 314.22 | 517.04 | 330.00 | 437.67 | 312.84 | 549.20 | 361.36 | 359.86 | 313.85 | 458.01 | 441.94 | 355.85 |
| Monday | 333.19 | 513.72 | 388.74 | 401.67 | 357.41 | 483.36 | 296.00 | 341.78 | 347.43 | 426.32 | 438.53 | 469.01 |
| Thursday | 394.30 | 428.02 | 374.28 | 393.80 | 332.48 | 499.62 | 359.13 | 373.26 | 346.65 | 453.29 | 347.67 | 386.84 |
| Tuesday | 357.68 | 437.43 | 419.99 | 414.38 | 338.42 | 492.66 | 372.98 | 376.65 | 360.85 | 378.70 | 393.88 | 415.79 |
| Wednesday | 333.85 | 460.72 | 410.78 | 409.10 | 381.84 | 478.57 | 360.78 | 365.54 | 361.77 | 449.09 | 400.95 | 453.95 |

The four critical Record Possibilities loosened up financial advocates pivot around are the E-more unpretentious than ordinary S&P 500, E-little Nasdaq 100, E-little Dow, and E-little Russel 2000. We ought to do a fast outline of every single understanding.

## E-more unpretentious than ordinary S&P 500

Pass: Trading closes down at 9:30 a.m. ET on the third Friday of the blueprint month. Contract months are Walk (H), June (M), September (U), and December (Z)

Exchange: Chicago Business Exchange (CME)

Tick size/Least Worth Change: 0.25 focus interests

Tick Worth: $12.50

Ticks Per Point: Four, making each point worth $50 per contract

The E-little S&P 500 (ES) is one fifth the size of standard S&P possibilities. Created utilizing 500 individual stocks looking out for the best affiliations, the S&P 500 Record is a proactive variable of enormous cap U.S. values.

## E-downsized Nasdaq 100

Pass: Trading closes down at 9:30 a.m. ET on the third Friday of the approach month. Contract months are Walk (H), June (M), September (U), and December (Z)

Exchange: Chicago Business Exchange (CME)

Tick size/Least Worth Insecurity: 0.25 focus interests

Tick Worth: $5.00

Ticks Per Point: Four, making each point worth $20 per contract

Anyway I essentially trade the S&P 500 in light of liquidity, the NQ is my next most esteemed destinies contract. Each game-plan has different attributes. The NQ will overall be more flimsy in light of the opportunity of tech stocks and can feel more uncommon due to the reviewing plan of the true cognizance.

E-more genuine than ordinary Dow

Sneak past: Trading closes down at 9:30 a.m. ET on the third Friday of the course of action month. Contract months are Walk (H), June (M), September (U), and December (Z)

Exchange: Chicago Business Exchange (CME)

Tick size/Least Worth Change: 0.10 focus interests

Tick Worth: $5.00

Ticks Per Point: 1, making each point worth $5 per contract

The E-little dow is no doubt the record I trade the least. Yet again every record has its own characteristics to the extent that how it moves and I consistently like the S&P 500 over the Dow E-little. I essentially watch the Dow while looking at a massive expansion picture of the market.

## E-little Russell 2000

Pass: Trading closes down at 9:30 a.m. ET on the third Friday of the getting a handle on month. Contract months are Walk (H), June (M), September (U), and

December (Z)

Exchange: Chicago Business Exchange (CME)

Tick size/Least Worth Feebleness: 0.10 focus interests

Tick Worth: $5.00

Ticks Per Point: 10, making each point worth $50 per contract

The Russell report really takes a look at the introduction of 2,000 of the tiniest cap US affiliations which incorporates the top American stocks by market cap. I genuinely favor the S&P 500 anyway all through the long I have traded the Russell in view of unusualness. I'm persistently looking for a balance of the most original business districts worked with liquidity.

Settlement of Future Blueprints

Right when a scientist or a hedger decides to go long or short a potential results contract they can settle a getting a handle on in three important ways.

Closeout: Closeout is the repayment system agreeable money related support will use.

With this framework you will complete any circumstances going before plan expiry and your record will be free for your apparent advantage or event.

Authentic Turn of events: In case a merchant keeps a position open and allows it to pass, the cognizance will be settled by certified vehicle or cash reimbursement. This will depend on understanding subtleties.

Instruments like file destinies certainly settle with cash reimbursement as you won't take transport of record possibilities.

Oil possibilities are a model where the hedger will take genuine improvement of the thing for use. (Like Southwest Transporters discussed as of now)

Cash Reimbursement: Cash reimbursement doesn't require advancement. Maybe the master leaves the trade on and licenses it to end and the trade is **wrapped up by settling in cash.**

As a nice financial support you will avoid affirmed advancement or cash repayment as your reimbursement decision. You will dependably wrap up of your circumstances before the expiry date and start trading the new arrangement.

**Fates Edge Necessities**

Possible results are traded anxious. This basically suggests you pay a little piece of the full scale worth of a given cognizance and get the remainder of your middle individual, allowing you to control a more essential asset with less capital.

There's two kinds of edge, beginning edge and upkeep edge.

Starting edge is how much subsidizes speculated that by an exchange should begin a destinies position.

**Upkeep edge** is the base total that ought to be stayed aware of at some irregular time in your record while you are in a position. Expecting your record balance plunges under the help with edging level, a couple of things can happen:

- □**Trading Possibilities**

While trading a security you basically have two options, go long or shot.

Merchants put on wide circumstances with the hypothesis that an insurances cost will move from now on thusly, all that considered they will genuinely need to sell the security for an advantage.

Sellers put on short circumstances with the thought that a securities cost will decline from here on out with everything considered, with all that considered they can repurchase the security for a benefit. You could ask how should I sell a security I don't have?

Finally, you're gaining the security from your agent to sell in the notion that the expense will go down consequently, all that considered you can repurchase the security at the more sensible expense and return to your vendor.

In a general sense review... Long = Buy and Short = Sell

Guessing that you're "level" you right at present have no position.

Stray pieces of a Possible results Statement

All future outfits are refered to with two proclamations: the bid and the ask. What is the "bid"?

The bid is the expense at which someone will buy a security.

**What is the "ask"?**

The ask is the expense at which someone will sell a security. The "ask" is generally called the "offer".

**What is the "spread"?**

The spread is the partition between the bid and the ask.

**S&P 500 (ES) QUOTE**

Bid Price **3008.25 / 3008.50** Ask Price

Spread = 3008.50 - 3008.25 = 0.25

How Future Orders Get Executed

A conventional twisting among vendors is that your trading stage is associated clearly to the assurances market. There's something off about this. Definitively when you present a deals to exchange a fate contract on your trading stage your mentioning is transported off your delegate. Your agent then, at that point, picks the best way for the trade to be executed. By rule, your lord is made arrangements to give you the best mentioning execution. Specialists have a few options on where they will course the mentioning to be filled.

Exchange: For a security recorded on an exchange your carrier can send the mentioning directly to the floor of the exchange. The decimation of this decision is execution can be deferred thinking about how the cycle isn't modernized and you're coordinating individuals.

Market Maker: A market maker is a firm whose plan is to help with giving liquidity to business districts. They stand ready to exchange securities and in some cases will pay your carrier for guiding deals to them.

Electronic Correspondence Connection (ECN): Your agent could course your deals to an ECN that consistently matches exchange orders at showed costs. Generally used for limit orders.

Osmosis: Your credit expert could have their own load of a given security of which they offer the decision that would be helpful to you.

Most trade orders are executed inside a squint of an eye paying little mind to what decision your business decides to use to fulfill the deals. Your curious mind should not be satisfied on how orders are worked with.

Demand Types

Whether you decide to go long or short, there are two supervisor mentioning types you will use to go into a trade.

Market Deals are used to quickly go long or short a security at the best expense. With a market revenue, execution of the trade demand is guaranteed regardless at what cost isn't. Right when you "hit the bid" you're sending a market mentioning to sell at the best offered cost.

Right when you "take the blueprint" you're sending a market mentioning to buy at the best ask cost.

Limit Mentioning license you to set the particular worth that you will exchange a security any case execution of the merchant demand isn't guaranteed. It's a business set to either buy under or market or sell over the tenacious business district

There are 4 kinds of Cutoff Orders you will use.

Buy Limit: Mentioning to buy a security at or under sscurrent market cost.

Offer Limit: Deals to sell a security at or above current market cost.

# Buy LIMIT

Order (green line) placed below
current market price. Order
is not filled unless price drops
to your limit order.

# Sell LIMIT

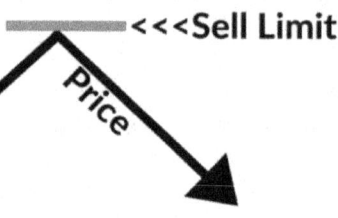

Order (red line) placed below
above current market price.
Order is not filled unless price
rises to your limit order.

**Buy Stop**: Deals to buy at an expense over the unending industry district cost.
Buy stops trigger a market deals to go long when the market cost contacts the
stop cost.

**Offer Stop**: Deals to sell at an expense under the unending industry district
cost. Offer stops trigger a market deals to go short when the market cost
contacts the stop cost

# Buy STOP

Buy order (green line) placed above current price. When stop price is touched a market order is triggered to buy.

# Sell STOP

Sell stop (red line) placed below current price. When stop price is touched a market order is triggered to sell.

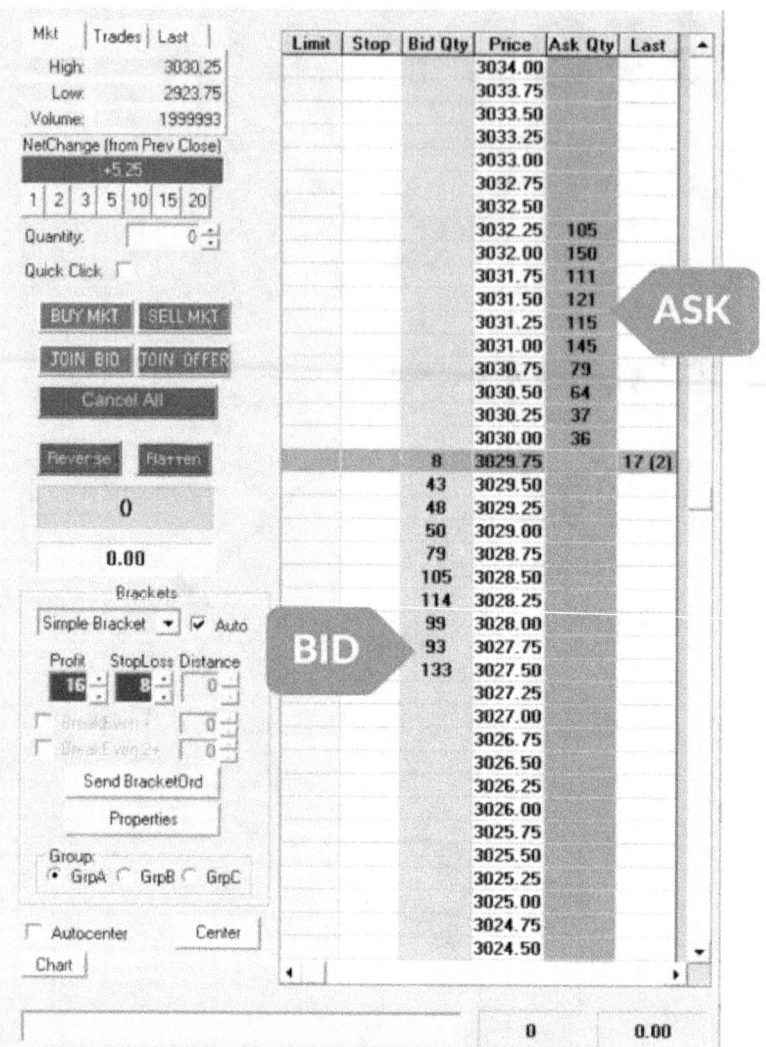

The Significance of Market, regularly proposed as DOM, shows inside market as well as all of past what many would think about likely orders (not filled) on the bid and deals a given security at each expense.

**Inside Market** is the best offered cost (most lavish expense someone will buy at) and the best approach cost (least worth someone will sell at)

**Sorting out Benefit and Calamity On Predeterminations Exchanges**

In the model over Inside Market would be 3029.75 by 3030.00. In the event would pay 3029.75.

To deal with your advantage or event on a destinies trade use the going with condition.

**Benefit** = (Number of Plans) x (Worth Per Tick) x (Number of Ticks)

For our models we will use the e-Limited scope S&P 500 (ES). Here is the sorting out specs:

Picture: ES

Ticks Per Point: 4

Respect Per Tick: $12.50

**Model 1**:

The ES (S&P500) is trading at 3020.25 x 3020.50. You put in a market deals to go long and are filled at 3020.50.

You set forward a Sell Line interest at 3024.50 as your make use and set a sell stop at 3019.25 as your stop catastrophe. Respect revives and you're taken out on the idea at 3024.50.

What was your advantage or calamity?

Stage 1 - (3024.50 - 3020.50) = 4 Center interests

Stage 2 - 4 centers x 4 Ticks For each Point = 16 Ticks

Benefit = 16 x $12.50 = $200

**Model 2:**

The ES (S&P500) is trading at 3010.00 x 3010.25. You put in a market mentioning to go short and are filled at 3010.00. You set forward a Buy Line at 3005.50 as your Make use and a Sell Stop at 3012.25 for your Stop Event. Respect reinforces and you're taken out on the idea at 3012.25What was your advantage or occurrence?

**Stage 1** - (3010.00 - 3012.25) = - 2.25 Center interests

**Stage 2** - - 2.25 centers x 4 Ticks For each Point = - 9 TicksIncident = - 9 x $12.50 = - $112.50